AN APPROACH

TO

SIGHT READING RHYTHM

BY

CARSON H. SHARP

The development of the ability to read simple and complex rhythms

AT FIRST SIGHT

For instrumental (band, orchestra, keyboard, etc.) and choral students.

For use by individuals and groups.

COPYRIGHT 2014 CARSON H. SHARP

Acknowledgments

In great appreciation to the following individuals who have been very instrumental in the development of these teaching materials:

To the students I have taught since I began teaching in 1956, many of whom have encouraged me to publish this material;

To Kirk Jones, whose encouragement and substantial help, insights, creativity, and computer skills have made the publication of this work possible;

To Clifford, Douglas, and Alan Sharp, who have motivated me to see this project to completion and provided invaluable help to that end.

And most importantly to my wife, Julia, who has without reservation supported me in my professional career.

Original Artwork by
Leo Platero

http://csharpstudios.weebly.com

CARSON H. SHARP

TROMBONE INSTRUCTOR
    Naval School of Music, Washington D. C. (1956-'59)

BRASS FACULTY
    Brigham Young University, Provo, Utah (1959-'63, 1968-'75)

DIRECTOR OF BANDS
    Delta Jr. & Sr. High Schools, Delta, Utah (1963-'65)

PROFESSIONAL PERFORMANCE
    Southern California, (1966-'67)

MEMBER - TROMBONE SECTION
    Utah Symphony Orchestra, Salt Lake City, Utah (1967-'69)

FACULTY MEMBER
    National Music Camp, Interlochen, Michigan (Summers 1970-'73)

PRIVATE TEACHING STUDIO - FREELANCE TROMBONE PERFORMANCE
    Salt Lake City, Utah, (1969-'85)

BRASS FACULTY
    Weber State College, Ogden, Utah (1975-'80)

BRASS FACULTY
    University of Utah, Salt Lake City, Utah (1981-'84)

DIRECTOR OF BANDS
    Whitehorse Jr. & Sr. High Schools, Montezuma Creek, Utah (1985-'94)

MASTER TEACHER - TROMBONE
    Tuacahn Center for the Arts, St. George, Utah (1993-'96)

BRASS FACULTY
    Utah Valley State College, Orem, Utah (1994-'99)

BRASS FACULTY
    Ricks College, Rexburg, Idaho (1995-'99)

DIRECTOR OF BANDS
    Mexican Hat Elementary, Mexican Hat, Utah (1999-2006)

PRIVATE TEACHING   To Present Day

Table of Contents

i   Introduction

ii   Words of Explanation

iii   Rhythm Symbols

Section 1   Quarter Notes, Rests, etc.

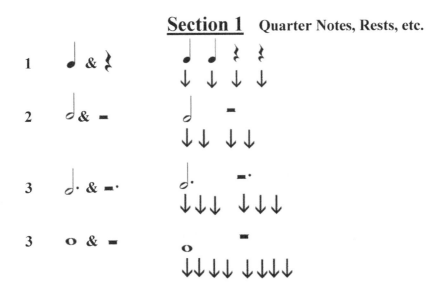

4&5   Practice Exercises with Time Signatures

Section 2   Eighth Notes, Rests, etc.

7   Dividing the Basic Beat into 2 Parts

12-14   Practice Exercises with Time Signatures

Section 3   Sixteenth Notes, Rests, etc.

15   Dividing the Basic Beat into 4 Parts

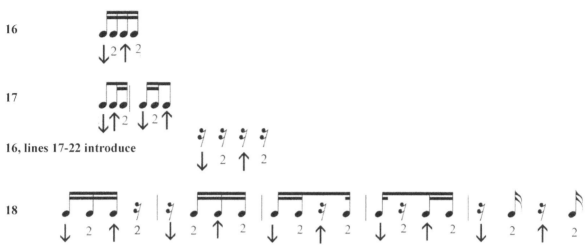

16, lines 17-22 introduce

19

20

21

22   Practice Exercises with Time Signatures and Ties

23   Comparative Meter Chart

Section 4 Triplet Eighth Notes, etc.

25   Dividing the basic beat into 3 parts

26

27   ♩. = 1 beat 6/8

Section 5 Combining Subdivisions of 2, 3, & 4

28 & 29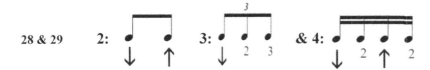

Section 6 Different Notes as the Basic Beat

30   ♩ = 1 beat (2/2) ₵

31   ♪ = 1 beat 2/8

32   Practice Exercises

Section 7   Other Rhythmic Figures

33-34   Quarter Note Triplets

Sixteenth Triplets & Thirty Second Notes

35   ♩ = 1 beat

36   ♩. = 1 beat

Whole & Sixteenth Notes as the Basic Beats

37   Lines 1-5

Mixed Meters

37   Lines 6-13, The Note Values Remain Constant

38   The Beat Remains Constant

Half Note Triplets & Subdivisions of 5 & 7

39   Half Note Triplets and Subdivisions of 5 & 7

40   Half Note Triplets, Lines 1-7

40   Subdivisions of 5 & 7, Lines 8-12

INTRODUCTION

One of the most valuable skills musicians can acquire is that of being able to <u>read at first sight</u> all (or most) of the music they are asked to play.

Sight reading is a skill that enables the student to make the most out of the time available to sing or play an instrument. The student can use the time otherwise spent on working out "rhythm" problems, to increase musicality and will be able to cover more literature. And every professional musician knows that the "musician who reads gets the jobs."

It's also true that the better the members of any school or other musical group sight read, the better that group will sound. This is true for several reasons:
<u>First</u>, more time can be spent on the development of other aspects of quality performing (sound, balance, intonation, and other general musicianship skills).
<u>Second</u>, the time involved in reaching an acceptable performance level is less, so the music will naturally be more interesting to the performer. And this "freshness" will show up dramatically in the concert or festival.
<u>Third</u>, the director will now be able to use more rehearsal time to teach some of the things (theory, music history, conducting, composition, etc.) that he or she "just didn't have time for" previously.

The more each student understands about music as a whole, the bigger their contribution will be to the group. Of course the greatest benefit will go to the individual student. The enjoyment of music will be enhanced considerably as a result of the skills gained in the reading of new music. It's been my experience that students, at a very young age (at least by the sixth grade) are capable of handling the concepts and skills required for effective sight reading.

There are of course, several areas in which skills must be developed before a student will be able to sight read well. The skill I'll focus on in this book is rhythm. This book is an extremely effective method for helping students develop the ability to read simple and complex rhythms at first sight.

The most effective way of developing the skill of instantly analyzing complex rhythmic figures is pulse subdivision. The difficulty most of us have had involves the material available to help us teach these concepts. Once the student understands what to do, practice material is needed that will help integrate each new concept into their bag of performance skills. Material is needed that will allow focus on a particular new concept without the distraction of other playing problems. Enough material is needed to avoid going over and over the same exercises. (The student can't learn to sight read if the material is familiar).

The manner in which this method solves this problem is with many lines of "single pitch" exercises. These exercises allow the student to concentrate on developing particular skills without having to worry about changes in pitch, etc. There are also enough exercises so that by the time all of them are covered, the previous exercises are forgotten and can be reused if necessary.

When used by instrumental organizations (bands and orchestras) or choral groups, choose a single pitch or octaves. Example: Concert F
Piano students (who use their feet on pedals) can v<u>ocalize</u> the ♩: say 'down' on each quarter note and rest. Instrumentalists not using their mouths to generate sound can vocalize the pulse (percussion, strings, etc.). If fingers are available to generate the pulse (vocalists), use them against your leg or lap to generate the pulse.

WORDS OF EXPLANATION

The following is given for the purpose of stating the author's reasons for advocating certain unorthodox procedures in the development of a student's rhythmic skills.

In applying this material it will be observed that toe tapping is advocated (This refers to a silent, unobvious movement of the toes, not to the bouncing of the forepart of the foot on the floor). The purpose of the toe tapping is to give the beginning student a tool with which to keep track of an even, constant pulse for the basic beat. The student should also be taught, and reminded as necessary, that his/her version of the pulse must agree with the director's when playing in a musical organization.

It will be observed that measures containing various numbers of beats, without meter signatures, are used in the exercises. The quarter note is used as the basic beat in all measures without meter signatures. This has been done to keep the student from assuming that all measures have the same number of beats. It is believed that this approach will keep students flexible in their approach to meter.

The use of meter (time) signatures is not discussed until the "Simple-Compound Meter Supplement" between lessons three and four. It is assumed that students will be studying out of a method book con-currently with their use of this rhythm study. The explanation of the meter signatures found in the student's method book is left to the discretion of the teacher.

It will, also, be observed that a syllabic system is not used in teaching the student to subdivide. It has been the author's experience that when the purpose is to develop MAXIMUM SIGHT READING SKILLS, the more direct approach of using a numeric system to subdivide the basic beat is best.

Emphasis in this approach is on <u>one beat and its subdivisions</u> at a time, not on its inclusion in a complete measure. By the time a student needs, for musical purposes, to emphasize primary and secondary accents in a measure, their rhythmic reading skills will be internalized.

It is extremely important that the material covered in a particular lesson be immediately applied to melodic material. Once the student can demonstrate the ability to read at sight rhythms found in a particular lesson, he or she should be encouraged to practice reading material of similar difficulty from method books, solos, etudes, etc., written for the instrument. Then, and only then, should the student move on to the next level.

Rhythm Symbols

Name	It's like $	Note Symbol	Rest Symbol	Representative Number
Whole	(dollar bill)	𝅝	𝄻	1 (1/1)
Half	(half dollar coin)	𝅗𝅥	𝄼	2 (1/2)
Quarter	(quarter coin)	♩	𝄽	4 (1/4)
Eighth	No Equivalent	♪	𝄾	8 (1/8)
Sixteenth	No Equivalent	𝅘𝅥𝅯	𝄿	16 (1/16)

Each rest symbol equals in silence the length of the note symbol bearing the same name.

Each successive note or rest is one-half the value of the preceding note or rest.

A dot placed behind any note adds one-half the value of that note to itself.

𝅝. = 𝅝 + 𝅗𝅥   𝅝.. = 𝅝 + 𝅗𝅥 + ♩

𝅗𝅥. = 𝅗𝅥 + ♩   𝅗𝅥.. = 𝅗𝅥 + ♩ + ♪

♩. = ♩ + ♪   ♩.. = ♩ + ♪ + 𝅘𝅥𝅯

♪. = ♪ + 𝅘𝅥𝅯   ♪.. = ♪ + 𝅘𝅥𝅯 + 𝅘𝅥𝅰

Section 1

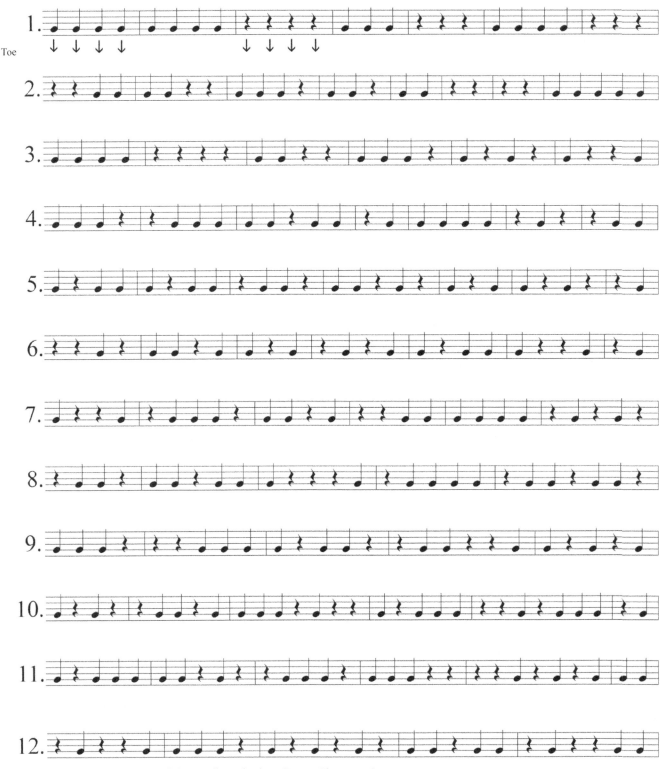

These exercises add time signatures. Count as before, and ignore the time signatures.

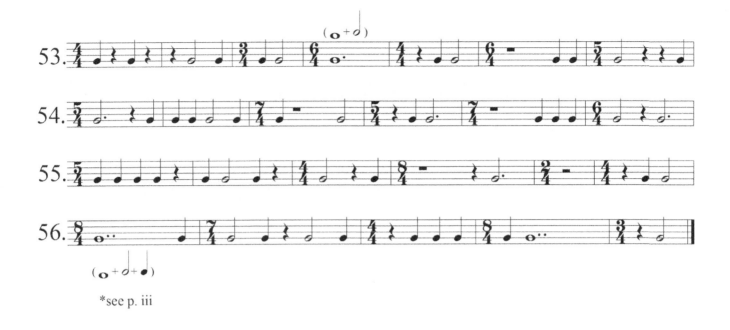

*see p. iii

Section 2

Dividing the basic beat into 2 parts

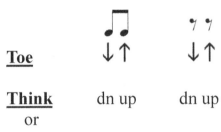

Toe

Think
or
Vocalize   dn up   dn up

Emphasizing equal <u>down</u> <u>up</u> movements gives the student a solid sense of the subdivision of the beat.

As more complex rhythms are encountered, they can be tied into the 'down up' subdivision. <u>No more involved</u> physical movement is necessary. (See Sections 3 – 7)

An Approach to Sight Reading Rhythm, Carson Sharp   12

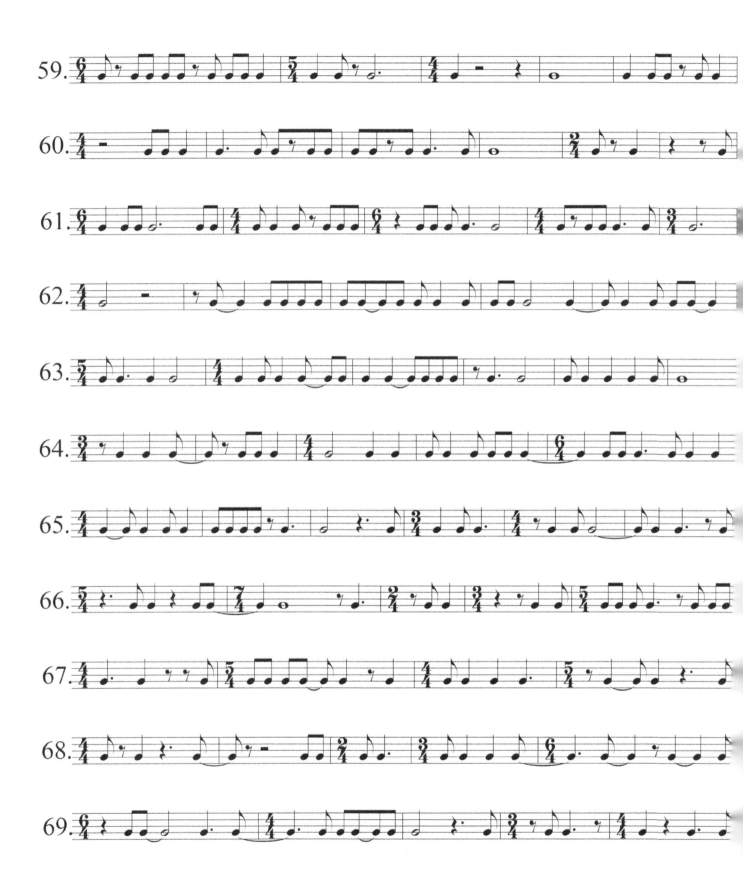

(o+ . + ♪)   (o+ . + ♪)

*see p. iii

An Approach to Sight Reading Rhythm, Carson Sharp   14

Section 3

Dividing the basic beat into 4 parts

Toe ♪♪♪♪ ❼❼❼❼
 ↓ 2 ↑ 2 ↓ 2 ↑ 2

Think   dn 2 up 2 dn 2 up 2
or
Vocalize

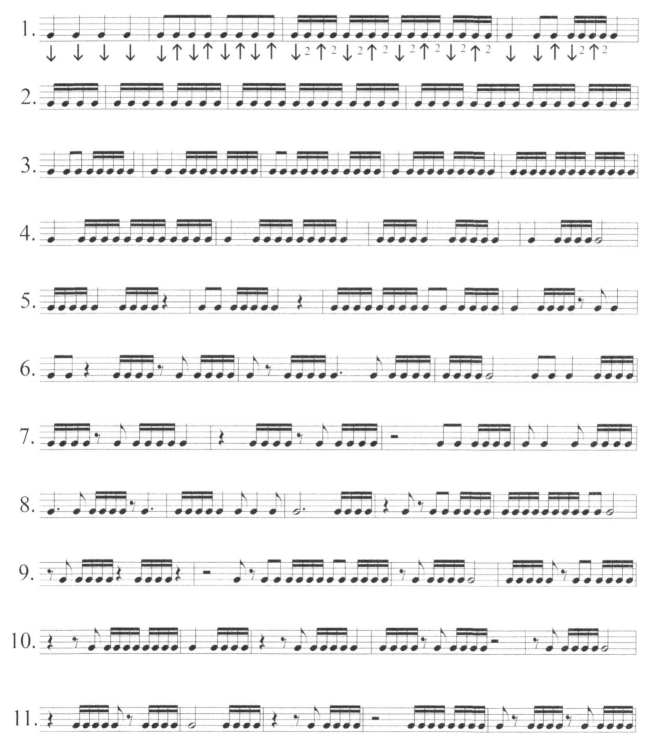

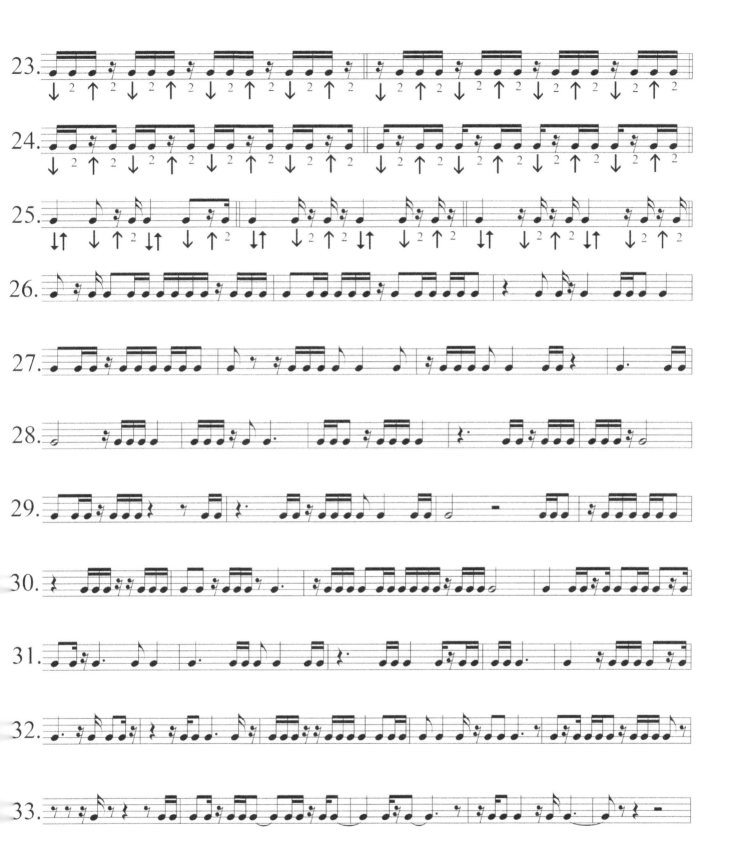

An Approach to Sight Reading Rhythm, Carson Sharp   18

An Approach to Sight Reading Rhythm, Carson Sharp   19

COMPARATIVE METER CHART

The information on this chart should be introduced at the teacher's discretion

SIMPLE	COMPOUND
A. Defined as: Basic Beat divided into two equal background beats. 1. ♩ = Basic Beat ♫ = Background Beats 2. ♩ = Basic Beat ♩♩ = Background Beats	A. Defined as: Basic beat divided into three equal background beats. 1. ♩. = Basic Beat ♫♪ = Background Beats 2. ♩. = Basic Beat ♩♩♩ = Background Beats
B. Time or meter signature 1. 4 = number of Basic beats per measure — 4 = type of note unit that receives 1 basic beat 2. Note units used for basic beat: 𝄁 o 𝄁 o. ♩ ♩ ♪ ♪ etc. 3. Note units used for background beats: o ♩ ♩ ♪ ♪ etc.	B. Time or meter signature 1. 6 = number of background beats per measure — 8 = type of note unit that receives 1 background beat. 2. Note units used for Basic beat: 𝄁 o. 𝄁 o. ♩. ♩. ♪. ♪. etc. 3. Note units used for background beats: o ♩ ♩ ♪ ♪ etc.
C. Examples of meter (time) signatures Slow 1. 3/8 ♫♪ | ♩. | ♪♪♪ | ♪ = 1 beat Each measure contains 3 eight notes or the equivalent. 2. 4/4 ♩♩♩♩ | ♩ ♩ | ♩ = 1 beat Each measure contains 4 quarter notes or the equivalent. 3. 2/4 ♩ ♩ | ♩ | ♩ 𝄽 | ♩ = 1 beat Each measure contains 2 quarter notes or the equivalent. 4. 3/2 ♩ ♩ ♩ | ♩ ♩ ♩ | ♩ = 1 beat Each measure contains 3 half notes or the equivalent.	C. Examples of meter (time) signatures Fast 1. 3/8 ♩. | ♫♪ | ♫♪ | ♩. = 1 beat Each measure contains 3 eighth notes or the equivalent. 2. 6/8 ♩. | ♫♫ | ♩. | ♩. = 1 beat Each measure contains 6 eighth notes or the equivalent. 3. 12/4 ♩♩♩♩. ♩♩♩♩♩| o. ♩. ♩. | Each measure contains 12 quarter notes or the equivalent. ♩. = 1 beat 4. 9/16 ♪ ♩. | ♬♬♬ ♪ | ♪ = 1 beat Each measure contains 9 sixteenth notes or the equivalent. To determine the number of beats per measure, divide 3 into the top number.

Some music contains measures with various meter (time) signatures

5. 4/4 ♩ ♩ ♩ ♩ \| ♩ ♩ ♩ \| 3/4 ♩ ♩ ♩ \| ♩. \| 2/4 ♫ ♩ \|

6. 3/8 ♩. ♩. \| ♩. \| 3/8 ♩. ♫♪ \| 3/8 ♫♪ \| ♫♪ \|

7. 3/4 ♩ ♩ ♩ \| 3/8 ♫ \| 4/4 ♩ ♩ \| 3/8 ♩. \| ♫♪ \| 3/4 ♩ ♩ \| 4/4 o \|

An Approach to Sight Reading Rhythm, Carson Sharp

Section 4

Dividing the basic beat into 3 parts

Page 26

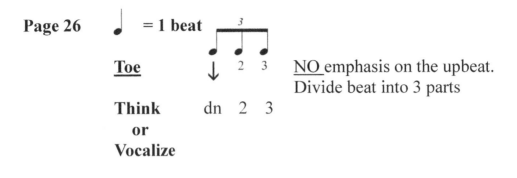

Page 27

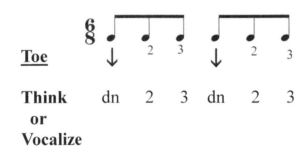

♩. = 1 beat.
Each note's length is determined by its relationship to a ♩.

♩. = 1 beat; ♩. = 2 beats; ♪♪♪ = 1-2-3

*To add sixteenth notes, see page 36, lines 13-15.

Section 5

Each ♩ (as indicated by the meter signature) = 1 basic beat.
Each note's length is determined by its relationship to the basic beat.
Think ↓↑, ↓23, or ↓2↑2 depending on the rhythmic figure to be played.

An Approach to Sight Reading Rhythm, Carson Sharp

Section 6
Half Note as Beat Unit

Eighth Note as Beat Unit

Practice Exercises

**Each line of these exercises uses a different note unit as the basic beat.
Each note's length is determined by its relationship to the note unit receiving the basic beat for that line. Play at least 2 lines at a time to practice moving from one meter to a different meter quickly.**

An Approach to Sight Reading Rhythm, Carson Sharp

Section 7
Other Rhythmic Figures
Quarter Note Triplets

QUARTER NOTE TRIPLETS

Developmental Steps

    A. Play accents (>) as marked on each ↓ beat.

    B. Accent every other note as marked
       Play several times to develop this skill.

    C. Use ties as marked. Articulate only accented notes.

    D. Apply to quarter note triplets ♩ ♩ ♩.

Lines 4-12:   Combining ♩ ♩ ♩ with other rhythms.

Sixteenth Triplets & Thirty Second Notes

Whole Note & Sixteenth Note = Basic Beat

Mixed Meters
The Note Values Remain Constant

An Approach to Sight Reading Rhythm, Carson Sharp

The Beat Remains Constant

HALF NOTE TRIPLETS

Developmental Steps

    A. 1ˢᵗ measure
        Play accents as marked.
        Repeat measure as needed

    B. 2ⁿᵈ measure
        Use ties as marked. Articulate only accented notes.
        Repeat measure as needed.

    C. 3ʳᵈ measure
        Apply to half note triplets 𝅗𝅥 𝅗𝅥 𝅗𝅥 (3).

P. 40   Lines 2-7 Combining 𝅗𝅥 𝅗𝅥 𝅗𝅥 (3) with other rhythms.

SUBDIVISIONS OF 5 AND 7

    Practice dividing the beat into various parts.
- Establish a steady beat (pulse) ♩ = 60 (or slower) <u>use metronome</u>
Vocalize the following on each beat until evenly distributed through each beat. Repeat on instrument.

    ↓   ↓   ↓   ↓
    1 2 3 4 5 1 2 3 4 5 1 2 3 4 5 1 2 3 4 5 etc.

- Establish a steady beat (pulse) ♩ = 60 (or slower) <u>use metronome</u>
Vocalize the following on each beat until evenly distributed through each beat. Repeat on instrument.

    ↓   ↓   ↓   ↓
    1 2 3 4 5 6 7 1 2 3 4 5 6 7 1 2 3 4 5 6 7 1 2 3 4 5 6 7 etc.

Apply to lines 8-12, p.40

Half Note Triplets

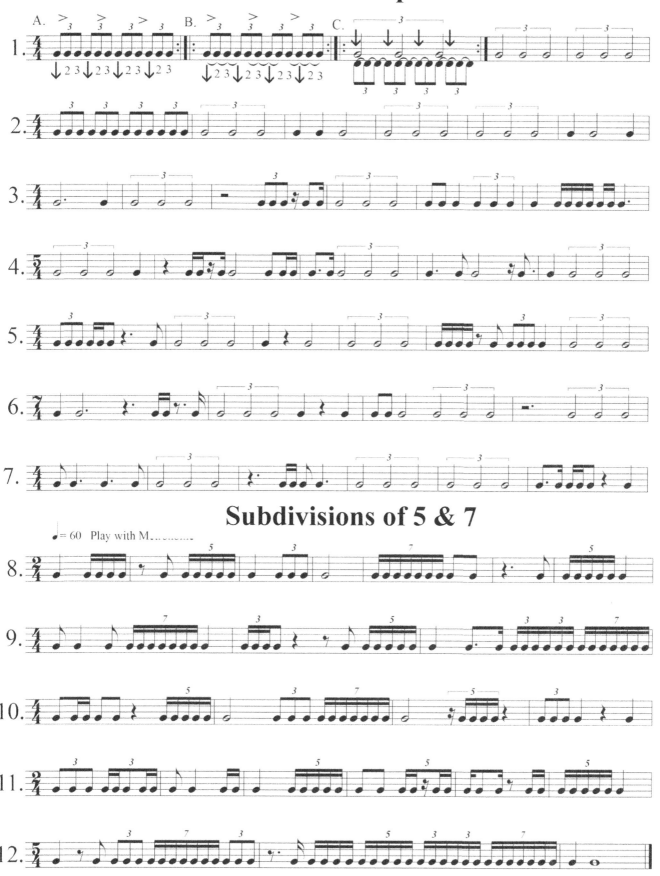

Subdivisions of 5 & 7

An Approach to Sight Reading Rhythm, Carson Sharp

Made in the USA
Coppell, TX
12 March 2024

30013081R00031